# Australia-Banaba Relations

## The Price of Shaping a Nation

Stacey M. King

BANABAN VISION PUBLICATIONS

Gold Coast, Australia

Australia Banaba Relations: the price of shaping a nation.
Copyright © Stacey M. King.
All rights reserved.
Published by Banaban Vision Publications
PO Box 1116 Paradise Point. Qld. 4216. Australia
www.banabanvision.com

 A catalogue record for this work is available from the National Library of Australia

ISBNs: Paperback: 978-0-6451491-4-2
Ebook: 978-0-6451491-5-9

This book may not be reproduced in any form or by any electronic or mechanical means, including information storage and retrieval system, without permission in writing from the authors. The only exception is a reviewer who may quote short excerpts in a review.

Cover designed by Stacey King

This content was written by the author and presented at:
The Pacific in Australia - Australia in the Pacific conference QUT, Carseldine campus, Brisbane, Australia 24 to 27 January 2006.

The author has provided information sourced from original documents, photographs and interviews either owned or kindly donated to the author. All other reference material has been sourced as quoted. Internal diagrams were created and/or supplied by the author.

# DEDICATION

Raobeia Ken Sigrah

1956-2021

Banaban Clan spokesman and historian

Your name will live on in history as a true Banaban warrior and a proud descendant of his people, who gave your people the greatest gift:

"Hold your head high and be forever proud of being BANABAN and ensure Banaban identity is never lost but passed on to future generations".

*"When I'm asked, Where is Banaba?
I reply, Scattered all over Australia."*
Banaban, Raobeia Ken Sigrah.


*"Over 13 million tons of Banaban land and the crushed bones of their ancestors have been scattered over Australian farmlands."*
Stacey King.

# Contents

Introduction .................................................................... 1
1. Australia's early phosphate mining history ..................... 3
2. Australia's role in discovery of Banaba phosphate ...... 5
3. Australia's role in the early mining of Banaba ............. 9
4. The effects of mining on the Banabans ......................... 11
5. Banaba under the Nauru Agreement ............................. 17
6. A World at War ......................................................... 21
7. Banabans forced removal from their homeland ........... 23
8. Japanese surrender to Australian forces on Banaba .... 27
9. Global changes in a post-war world and Australia's acquisition of Christmas Island phosphate deposits .... 29
10. Australia and Nauru under a new Trusteeship Agreement ..................................................................... 31
11. The differences between Banaba, Nauru and Christmas Islands under the British Phosphate Commission .......... 35
12. The legal responsibilities of the British Phosphate Commissioners ....................................................... 39
13. Final close to phosphate mining ................................. 45
14. Summary ..................................................................... 47
13. Conclusion ................................................................. 55
References ....................................................................... 59
About the Author ........................................................... 65
Other Titles By The Author ........................................... 67

Appendix 1
Letter from Prime Minister Australia 1927 ........................ 64

# Photographs

1. Albert Ellis arrived on Banaba in 1900. He set up camp at Tabwewa.................................................................. 6
2. Albert Ellis, discovered that a rock that had been used as the office doorstop contained over 78 percent phosphate of lime in July 1899.................................................................. 8
3. Banaba (Ocean Island) was also under the Nauru Agreement.......................................................................... 16
4. 232 BPC staff and 823 Chinese labourers were evacuated aboard *Le Triomphant* to Australia. ................................... 22
5. Banaba (Ocean Island) under Japanese occupation........ 25
6. Japanese surrender to Australian Forces aboard........... 26
7. Devastating impact of phosphate mining by 1932. ....... 47
8. The ongoing destruction of Banaba by phosphate mining by 1968.................................................................... 48
9. Australia was the primary recipient of Banaba's phosphate............................................................................. 58

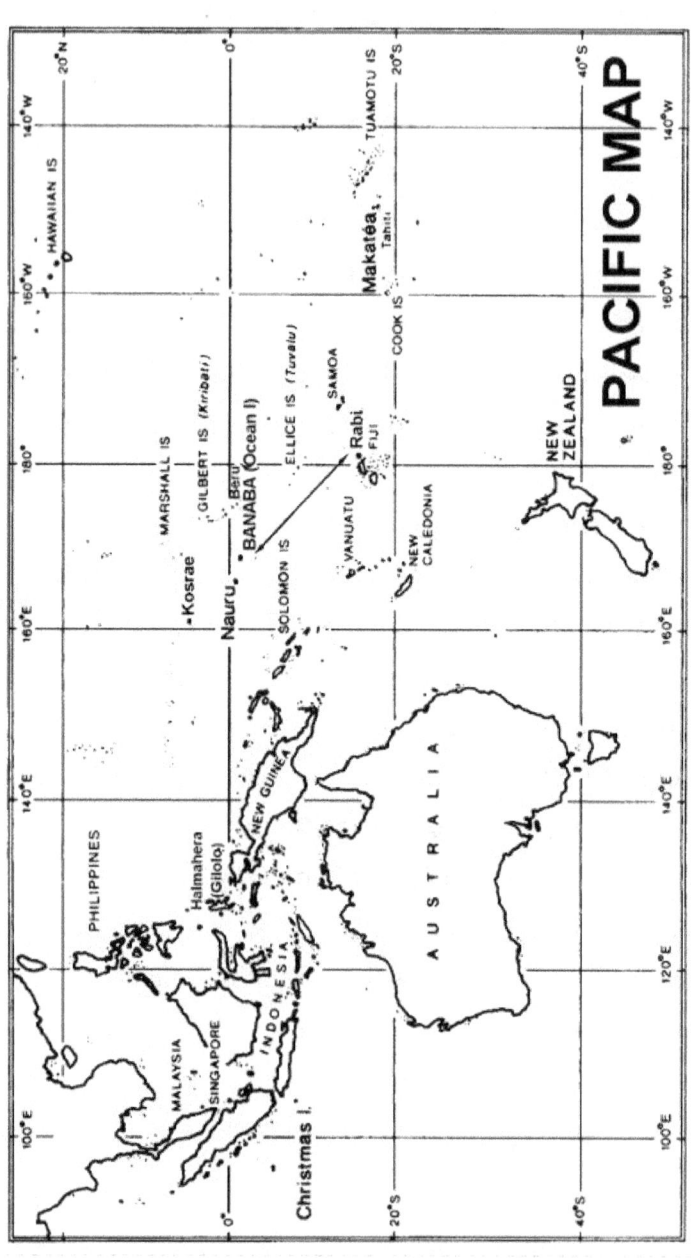

# Introduction

On November 25, 1979, the final shipment of phosphate left Ocean Island (now known as Banaba) aboard Cape Hawke for delivery to Australia, marking the end of a joint commercial venture between the governments of the United Kingdom, New Zealand, and Australia. This event brought closure for the Australian Government as a major stakeholder in the mining of Banaba. However, for the indigenous inhabitants of Banaba, it marked the devastating aftermath of eighty years of mining and their forced removal to Rabi Island, over 2,000km away in Fiji. More than forty years later, this episode of history remains largely forgotten by the Australian Government and the general population.

By analysing the critical historical events during the phosphate mining and subsequent fertiliser industry, the Banabans are calling on the Australian Government to recognise their significant contribution in aiding Australia's wealth as an agricultural nation. At the turn of the last century, only 450 indigenous Banabans stood in the way of a new discovery that was about to revolutionise the Australian fertiliser industry. While the

Australian Government took over one-third ownership of Banaba's phosphate reserves and all the associated financial benefits that followed, they have never accepted any accountability for their actions in destroying Banaba and nearly annihilating its people. Throughout this episode of history, the Australian Government has used political expediency and technicalities to manipulate and hide behind the mantle of the United Kingdom's sovereignty over Banaba. Yet Nauru, another phosphate island under the same commercial accords, has had the full recognition of the Australian Government.

The question remains: why has Banaba been left so politically polarised compared to Nauru when they were both originally acquisitions of the same company and subsequently the jewels in the crown of the governments of the United Kingdom, Australia, and New Zealand under the auspices of the Nauru Agreement?

# 1. Australia's early phosphate mining history

Before the discovery of phosphate on Banaba, Australia's early guano mining industry relied on scattered deposits throughout various islands along the coast of Queensland. John T. Arundel and Company, a British-owned company led by director John Arundel, believed that they had a God-given right to develop Pacific trading for the financial benefit of the Empire and the spiritual betterment of the indigenous populations.

In 1871, agricultural chemists discovered the significance of phosphorus in unlocking plant nutrients in soil. This discovery led to the development of a new fertiliser industry based on treating phosphate rock with sulfuric acid. While large rock and alluvial phosphate deposits had been discovered in the Americas, Morocco, and Tunisia, shipping costs and other economic factors left Australian and New Zealand farmers dependent on regional phosphate guano deposits.

By 1890, John T. Arundel and Company, which had been mining phosphate guano on tiny atolls across the Pacific, transferred their operations to Queensland's east coast, starting at Raine Island in the far northern section of the Barrier Reef. They then moved on to Rocky Island in the

Gulf of Carpentaria before focusing on the Capricorn Bunker group of islands off the central coast, beginning with Lady Elliot Island in 1893 and then moving on to Lady Musgrave Island and nearby Fairfax Island (Anon: 2005a). The only significant deposits for the Company's entire Queensland operation were those found at Heron Island and North West Island.

By 1897, the fertiliser industry in Australia and New Zealand was still in its infancy, with meagre quantities of low-grade phosphate guano assaying around 30 percent, while farmers demanded 60 percent (Ellis 1936:151). The Company was struggling to stay afloat. During this critical period, the Company made additional acquisitions, including properties and other trading opportunities in the Gilbert[1], Ellice, and Marshall Islands groups. It reconstituted its operations as the Pacific Islands Company (PIC).

---

[1] Gilbert and Ellis Islands are now known as the independent nations of Kiribati (pronounced Ki-ri -bus) and Tuvalu. The Kiribati people are referred to as I-Kiribaiti

# 2. Australia's role in discovery of Banaba phosphate

In July 1899, a young employee at the Company's Sydney office, Albert Ellis, discovered that a piece of fossilised rock that had been used as the office doorstop contained over 78 percent phosphate of lime. The sample was acquired during a previous trading trip to Pleasant Island (now known as Nauru), a German territory at the time. The Company's management planned to make a secret visit to both Nauru and another small island called Banaba to collect more samples without raising any suspicion from the inhabitants.

Banaba had been first sighted by Captain Jered Gardener in 1801, and Captain John Mertho officially claimed its discovery in 1804 and named it Ocean Island. The samples from Banaba that were collected by the Company in December 1899 assayed at between 84 and 86 percent phosphate of lime, the highest levels the Company had ever seen. The Company immediately set out to secure these deposits, and it was suggested to the Colonial Office that Banaba might be brought under Britain's Gilbert Islands Protectorate. However, the British

Government still needed to be convinced. After various meetings between the Company's director and the Western Pacific High Commissioner, it was suggested that the Company should make its own arrangements with the island's inhabitants.

1. Albert Ellis arrived on Banaba in 1900. He set up camp at Tabwewa.

Albert Ellis was sent to Banaba aboard the Archer and arrived on May 3, 1900. He quickly negotiated with the Banaban people and secured an agreement that gave the Pacific Island Company the sole right to Banaban rock and alluvial phosphate. The agreement also allowed the Company to erect buildings, lay tram lines, make roads, and construct jetties and shipping places on the island, with the provision that the Company would not remove phosphate where coconut or fruit trees were growing. However, the PIC would have the right to remove non-fruit-bearing trees which could interfere with their workings. Ellis agreed to pay the Banaban people a rate of fifty pounds per annum or trade to that value for a term of nine hundred and ninety-nine years.

Ellis soon realised he had to contend with four different villages containing four hundred and fifty people and amended his agreement by adding more signatures to the contract. The Banabans disputed the term 'Banaban village,' stating that they lived in *kainga* (extended family hamlets) that were scattered over the island in accordance with inherited land holdings. The idea of European-based village systems would be used in the years ahead to remove the Banabans from their ancestral lands and to try to bring about more control and order over the island's inhabitants.

Following the agreement, which would become known as the Scandalous Document, the PIC focused on getting the mining operations up and running on Banaba as soon as possible. The island had already been formally annexed to the British Empire, and the Company's interests were finally secured on September 28, 1901. The staff and mining plant were brought over from the Company's Queensland, North West Island operation. George Ellis (Albert's older brother) and five others arrived on Banaba from Australia by October of the following month.

2. Albert Ellis, discovered that a rock that had been used as the office doorstop contained over 78 percent phosphate of lime in July 1899.

# 3. Australia's role in the early mining of Banaba

Over the next year, while the first stages of the mining operations were being set up, Ellis had begun to grasp that his Colonial ideas of King and Chiefship had no bearing on the Banabans or their landholdings (Ellis 1936; Grimble 1956; Sigrah and King 2001). Quietly he busied himself negotiating with individual Banaban men and women for leases and land purchases and getting these contracts formalised and registered on the Government's Land Registry in Fiji. By 1904 after extensive negotiations with German Company, Jaluit Co., the Company reconstituted as the Pacific Phosphate Company (PPC) to take over the leases, licences and all other rights related to mining on Nauru as well. German financial interest in the new Company was considerable, and there was an agreement for Germans to be on the new Board, while two-thirds of the directors had to be British.

Australia's early involvement at this stage of Banaban history was mainly through the Company's Sydney based office and the staff at both management and supervisory level on Banaba. By 1904 the number of 'white' employees (as referred to by the Company) on Banaba were mainly from Australia and New Zealand and numbered fifty. This group supervised a labour force of more than 900 Islanders and a number of Japanese who had been recruited as mechanics, cooks and stewards. It was also during this period that the island's living conditions were no longer considered unrefined pioneering. Living conditions for the European staff had greatly improved, with some of the men's wives joining them. However, conditions in the field remained primitive, with most of the mining labour still being carried out by hand with picks and wheelbarrows. Even with this basic equipment and mining methods, the PPC could ship a total of 77,420 tons of phosphate for that year.

By 1905 the levels of phosphate shipped from Banaba had risen to 107,930 tons. Most of these shipments were sent to Australia for further processing into superphosphate. By 1906, despite the opposition of British directors, the Australian headquarters of the PPC were further expanded with the headquarters of the Company moved to Melbourne. This gave the Company immediate access to Colonial buyers and also the belief that there was a growing feeling that everything Australian was commercially good for business. A purely Australian office for the Company would reap benefits. It was decided to also keep the Sydney office. The next major historical events were in 1907, when the headquarters of the British Government was transferred to Banaba, and the PPC's first shipment of phosphate left Nauru.

# 4. The effects of mining on the Banabans

By 1909 the island had become even more civilised. The Banaban population was officially quoted as 400 to 500, while the rest of the status-graded population consisted of around 1,000 recruited Pacific Island labourers, mostly from the Gilbert and Ellice Islands Group, with 400 or more Japanese and 80 European company staff together with a small contingent of Fijian Police (Ellis 1936).

The Island's mining operations had also become fully industrialised with electrical lighting and machinery that was leading-edge technology. While the impact on the Island's environment was devastating, with mined-out areas left with impenetrable fields of towering limestone pinnacles. Even Mahaffy, the Island's Resident Commissioner, was alarmed and wrote memorandums to the Western Pacific High Commission in Fiji that a systematic land rehabilitation programme had to be implemented. To his amazement, Westminster informed him 'that the Company had every desire not to actin any way contrary to native interest' (Williams and Macdonald 1985:87). Soon after, Mahaffy was assigned to another overseas posting, and no rehabilitation was implemented. By this stage, the relationship between the Banabans and the Company had deteriorated to the stage that the Banabans were refusing to lease or sell any more of their land.

Uncomfortable questions were starting to be raised in the United Kingdom House of Parliament about the treatment of Banaban landowners. By 1912 the level of Banaban unrest on the Island was at a level where the Banabans now flatly refused to part with another square yard of their land unless it was taken by force. With this ultimatum, Resident Commissioner Captain Quayle Dickson had made the strongest representation to the Colonial Office on behalf of the oppressed Banaban landowners, only to find that the Company had brought enough pressure to bear for his removal from his post.

The year 1913 would prove another milestone and turning point for Banaban landowners. Up until this period, the PPC had to negotiate all land dealings with individual Banaban landowners under the Phosphate and Tree Purchase deeds (Maude 1946:4). The stalemate would finally be resolved when the Government and Company brokered another agreement with the 257 Banaban landowners to sell off another 146 acres (58.6 hectares). One main argument was the Banabans' claims and objection to the Company's use of inaccurate records of land features and measurements. Approximate measurements were no longer acceptable to them (Sigrah & King 2001:224).

The Banabans also claimed that the Company was switching leases from outside to inside mining boundaries. They were also concerned that the replanting of food-bearing trees was not proving practicable, especially during drought. This issue would not be officially addressed until 1931 when Maude was appointed by the Colonial Government as Native Land Commissioner. By this time, thirty-one years of illegal land acquisitions of Banaban lands would go unchecked.

The 1913 Agreement with the Banaban landowners, Government and PPC saw the land purchase payments rise from £40 to £60 an acre and compensation under the Phosphate and Tree Purchase deeds to remain the same. In addition, another royaltyof 6 pence a ton would be awarded on every ton of phosphate shipped from Banaba after July 1 1912.

The land purchase payments were to go direct to the Banaban landowners. All of the royalty payments accumulated between 1913 and1914, less £300 that had been deducted to start the Banaban Fund, were to be used for the benefit of the Banaban community. The funds could be used whichever way the Banaban Magistrate, known as *Kaubure*, recommended. However, it was still subject to the approval of the Resident Commissioner, who could endorse the expenditure as 'equitable and not wasteful'.

After 1914, the interest on the capital sum in the Banaban Fund was to be used and distributed annually 'among all Banabans who leased land to the Company' (Maude1946:5). Even though it was not a condition of the

1913 Agreement, payments were also made annually from the interest accruing from the Fund for the maintenance of Banaban services.

With the onset of World War One, minimal impact was felt on Banaba, especially on the mining operations, except for thirty-five European staff who returned to Australia and New Zealand to enlist. The Banabans, who were always in constant conflict with the Company, still believed they had an obligation to help the great King of England and sent a gift of 1,000 pounds to the Prince of Wales Relief Fund.

This period also afforded the PPC the opportunity of removing their German business partners and shareholders while the Company's German staff on Nauru was incarcerated in Australian prison-of-war camps. Behind the scenes, the war had become the catalyst for another significant episode in Banaba's history that would soon see Australia as a major stakeholder in the operation. Australia became a major stakeholder in the British Phosphate Commission.

As the war drew to a close, Australian Prime Minster William Hughes was in London for postwar talks, including the Allies retention of German possessions in the Pacific and discussions over proposed mandates. Originally it was proposed that New Zealand should have Western Samoa, Nauru should be brought within the jurisdiction of the Western Pacific High Commission, and German New Guinea should go to Australia. All the other islands previously under German control above the

Equator would go to Japan (Williams and Macdonald 1985:126). Hughes insisted that Nauru should be included in Australia's allocation.

After much debate, a compromise was finally reached on June 27 1919, where the three governments of Australia, New Zealand and the United Kingdom would share in the Mandate over Nauru, including acquiring the PPC's mining rights and assets. This complex and protracted agreement would be called the Nauru Agreement of 1919. Each of the three governments would be awarded the following allocations under Article 14 of the Agreement:

- United Kingdom: 42%
- Australia: 42%
- New Zealand 16%

This was on the provision that these allotments were for home consumption for agricultural purposes and not for export (Williams and Macdonald 1985:135).

By February 18 1920, the privately owned PPC was bought out by the three governments of the United Kingdom, Australia and New Zealand conjointly for the sum of £3.5 million and renamed the British Phosphate Commission (BPC). The Company management met for various talks in London to decide staff redundancies and new management positions, including the placement of three Commissioners to act as representatives for the governments involved in the new Commission. The new BPC agenda was to operate as a non-profit enterprise for the three governments. The Australian Prime Minister

(Billy) Hughes was naively stating in Australian Parliament that as far as the three governments were concerned, 'obliviously no political influence of any kind can be permitted'. However, for the Banabans, there were other discussions on the table regarding their future, with the Company's (now the Commission) management view that sooner rather than later, the Banabans had to be removed to another island on the grounds that 'it will benefit the natives and facilitate the operations of the Commission' (Williams and Macdonald 1985: 148).

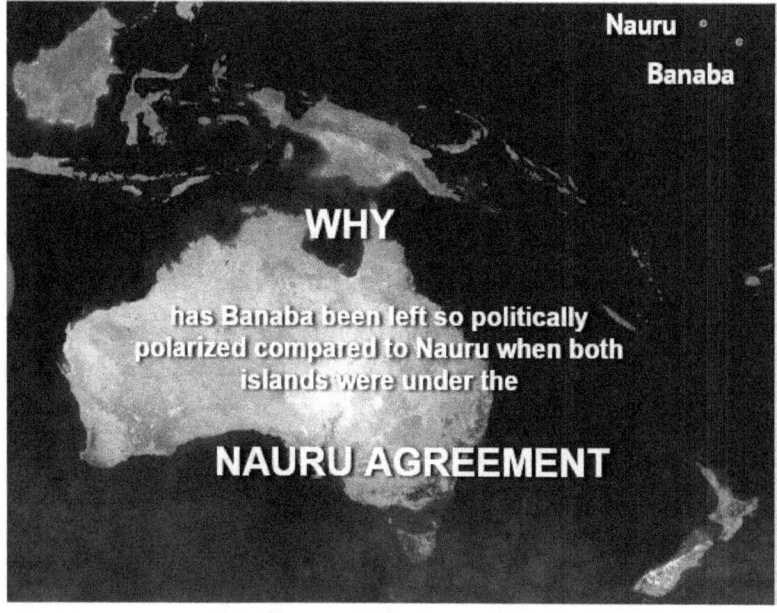

3. Banaba (Ocean Island) was also under the Nauru Agreement.

# 5. Banaba under the Nauru Agreement

The newly formed BPC had another problem to resolve over their other mining operations on Banaba which would now be running in competition. By June of the same year, this situation was rectified, with Banaba also included in the deal under the Nauru Agreement of 1919. It would soon become apparent that Article 14 would cause much consternation between the three governments. By 1924 shipped phosphate figures clearly showed the discrepancies in the original Agreement figures. From a total of 1.5 million tons, 950 000 tons had gone to Australia, 160 000 to New Zealand, and only 30 000 tons to Britain, while 360 00 tons had gone to Japan and other countries.

While the newly formed Commission was busy taking over their non-profit venture based on the land acquired under the 1913 Agreement, the Banaban landowners were adamant that no more land agreements would be entered into. The Banabans were completely unaware of the decisions these three powerful governments made to have them permanently removed from their homeland.

Australia's compliance in this has been uncovered in a decoded telegram by the Australian Governor-General to the Secretary of State for Dominion Affairs on behalf of the Australian Prime Minister dated October 22 1927 (see Appendix: 1 for the full version) and stating:

> 'As all the phosphate on Ocean Island will eventually be required, it appears to Commissioners advisable that steps should be taken to secure another island or islands for the use of the Banabans when Ocean Island is no longer suitable for their habitation and the Commissioners have expressed their willingness to co-operate in this matter'.

Even Maude, in 1946, endorsed that the Banabans removal from their Island had been on the agenda since 1914. He quoted that the Resident Commissioner of the time had stated, '... if the phosphate industry were to fail, the race would literally be blotted out of existence ...'.

Notably, this topic was raised after the Banabans first attempted to block any more land acquisitions prior to the 1913 Agreement.

In 1928 the situation had become critical between the Banabans and the newly formed BPC as previous leases became depleted. The Banabans stood firm, especially when they realised that the BPC was now using them to subsidise the farmers of Australia and New Zealand with cheap phosphate that was well under world market price and at the expense of their Island's land and food trees.

From the beginning of mining, it had become apparent that the Company's clause to replace their 'food bearing trees' had never been taken seriously. The Commission also stood fast, claiming the Banabans landowners were making unreasonable demands. This stalemate was abruptly resolved when the Colonial Government intervened by enacting new laws known as the Mining Ordinance No. 4of 1928. This enabled compulsory acquisitions of Banaba land (Maude 1946:5).

As these new laws came into force, any protests or actions by the Banabans were now deemed unlawful. Yet even with this in mind, the peaceful Banabans still refused to give in. As mining began around the lush plateau area of Buakonikai Village, Banaban women clung to their precious food trees so that the bulldozers would have to destroy them along with their trees.

The Government was quick to act and, not wanting to be involved or have any of the BPC staff implicated in such unsavoury business, released prisoners (mainly from the Gilbert Islands) from the Island's prison and quickly recruited them as acting police officers. Under instructionsand the supervision of Resident Commissioner Arthur Grimble, the women were physically removed by these now armed constables from their trees and also when they tried to approach representatives of the BPC.

This was a sad turning point in Banaban history when it was realised that new laws could be made. The Banabans had always been a lawful community who held respect for their Elders and the white men they called te

I-Matang. Over the thirty years since their arrival on the Island, the naïve Banabans finally realised that these te I-Matangs were only interested in destroying their land. While the governments of the United Kingdom, Australia and New Zealand hid behind the cloak of the British Phosphate Commission, the Commission also had the backing of the Colonial Office to see that new laws were implemented. The Colonial Office made a grave decision to ensure the new laws were enacted. They were prepared to allow the Banabans to be shot if needed.

By 1930 as the Banabans faced the reality of their situation and knew that they wouldhave to try and take their grievances further afield, other global events were evolving, with Australia and New Zealand in the grip of a depression. The lifestyle for European staff on Banaba was a welcome relief to what was being experienced back in their homelands. The BPC used this period as an opportunity to restructure and improve its operations on the Island.

# 6. A World at War

More ominous world events were looming with rumblings of War in Europe. By December 1940, events escalated when War came to the Pacific when two German raiders sunk two of the BPC's prized vessels, the *Triadic* and *Triaster,* off Nauru. This immediately put pressure on the Commission with reduced shipping operations and calls for the BPC to stop supplying Japan with phosphate until the demand for phosphate could be fully met for the Commissioned countries first. British Colonial officials were quick to criticise Australian and New Zealand politicians and businessmen who they stated were,

> 'prone to show an undue nervousness of the activities and capabilities of Japan in the Pacific… and pressing for the evacuation of European women and children from the phosphate islands' (Williams and Macdonald1985:308).

But by the beginning of 1942, American intelligence predicted that the Japanese were about to push southward into the Pacific. It was decided to evacuate BPC staff and Chinese labour as soon as possible. On February 28,

232 BPC staff and 823 Chinese labourers were evacuated aboard *Le Triomphant* to Australia, while the BPC's 713 Gilbert and Ellice Islands labourers and their families were left behind with the entire Banaban population.

4. 232 BPC staff and 823 Chinese labourers were evacuated aboard *Le Triomphant* to Australia.

# 7. Banabans forced removal from their homeland

While the Banabans enjoyed their first taste of freedom and the abandonment of phosphate mining on their Island, it would only be short lived. By August of the same year, 500 Japanese troops and 50 labourers had landed and taken over the Island by force. As the Banabans now struggled for survival under a new and even more dangerous adversary, they were unaware of contractual arrangements being carried out on their behalf back in Fiji.

While the rest of the world faced the ravages of War, it also afforded opportunities for others. Rabi Island in the northeast region of Fiji had been a freehold Island owned by Lever Brothers as a copra plantation. It was decided that with War in the Pacific, Fiji was expected to fall to the Japanese. With commercial interests in mind, Rabi was sold for A£25,000 to the Banabans (Maude 1946:11). While the Banabans were ignorant of these events, the Colonial Office negotiated and finalised the purchase using the Banaban's own Provident Fund to finance the deal.

Over the following months, the Banabans suffered greatly at the hands of the Japanese. By 1943, a year after the Japanese invasion and with grave food shortages, the Japanese removed all but 143 young men from the Island, sending the Banabans off to labour camps in Kosrae[2], Tarawa[3] and Nauru. Of the original 2,413 people who had remained on Banaba and were forcibly removed from the Island by the Japanese, almost 1,000 were Banabans. Dozens of other Gilbertese and Ellice Islanders had married into or been adopted by Banaban families and considered Banaba their home.

While the Banabans struggled for survival in the labour camps and as the War drew to a close, plans were made to collect the dispersed Banabans as soon as they were freed from Japanese hands and take them directly to Rabi Fiji.

Albert Ellis said, 'while there is obviously a great advantage in the Banabans being transferred directly to Rabi ... the matter will require careful handling'. The new High Commissioner, Sir Alexander Grantham, shared his opinion.

By July 1945, and with the Banabans having no knowledge of the plans being made for them, it had become very evident that the BPC Commissioners and the

---

[2] Kosrae also traditionally known as Kusaie is now under the Federate States of Micronesia.
[3] Tarawa is the main island in the Gilbert Group (now the Republic of Kiribati

United Kingdom officials were totally focused on resuming mining as soon as possible.

5. Banaba (Ocean Island) while under Japanese occupation 1942-45.

6. Japanese surrender to Australian Forces aboard Diamantina1 1945.

# 8. Japanese surrender to Australian forces on Banaba

On September 3 1945, the Americans handed over control of the southwest Pacific region to the British. The formal Japanese surrender of Banaba and Nauru was to be accepted by the Australians, with the BPC Commissioners also present abroad Australia's H.M.A.S. *Diamantina* (Ellis 1946). Other BPC staff and Civil Administration accompanied the expedition.

Their mission was to focus totally on the rehabilitation of the mining facilities. They discovered that Banaba's bomb damage was far less than on Nauru, with about one-third of the BPC and governmentinstallations needing to be replaced. It seemed that the Japanese marines that had been stationed on Banaba had kept the Island in far better order and that the total Banaban population had left the Island, and their villages had been destroyed.

However, it is during this period that the European version of history starts to differ from that of the Banabans, citing that 'all the Banaban villages had been destroyed by the Japanese during the war' and the

'Banabans could not return to Banaba as there was nowhere on the Island to accommodate them'. Evidence has emerged that many of the Banaban pre-war houses were still standing and did still exist. Fifty years later, these accusations were endorsed by pre and post-war BPC staff. The Japanese had kept all the staff houses in good working order during their occupation and never destroyed the villages. In fact, some of these informants have quoted that they believe the Australian Occupation Force was responsible for destroying Banaban houses under instruction from the United Kingdom Government.

By the time of the invasion, many of the Banaban village houses were made of timber and corrugated iron, like other European style houses built on the Island. The late Rabi elder, Keith Christopher, also verified this fact during an interview with the authors in 1997. He stated that while on an official trip to Banaba in the 1960s with mining at its peak, he was shocked to discover his old house still standing in Tabiang village with BPC Gilbertese staff occupying his home (Sigrah and King 2001:261-264). When asked why he did not report this fact to authorities, he simply replied, 'because I am a Banaban, and noone wanted to listen'.

The Banabans agree that by the end of the War, 349 Banabans, Gilbertese and Ellice labourers had died or been murdered on Banaba during the Japanese occupation. On December 15 1945, 703 Banabans and 300 Gilbertese arrived on Rabi, Fiji, aboard the British Phosphate Commission's S.S. *Triona.*

# 9. Global changes in a post-war world and Australia's acquisition of Christmas Island phosphate deposits

A number of significant developments during the War and in the immediate post-war years would bring about a great deal of change for the British Phosphate Commission. Up until this period, the Commission had enjoyed control over the phosphate industry. The formation of the United Nations to replace the discredited League of Nations was brought about in an effort to bring about peace and guarantee fundamental human rights for all people, whatever their existing political status, especially concerning the plight of colonial peoples.

Banaba and Nauru now came under the scrutiny of the United Nations, and soon political factors began to outrank commercial considerations. The Commissioners believed that the only solution to protect the future of the mining industries on Banaba and Nauru was through resettlement schemes and trust investments for the indigenous landowners.

As part of the BPC distribution activities, stockpiles of phosphate had been maintained at superphosphate manufacturing plants throughout Australia and New Zealand. During wartime shortages, this proved very successful but also emphasised the total dependence of agricultural industries in Australia and New Zealand on importing raw materials to manufacture fertiliser. Due to this factor, the Commissioners decided on the acquisition of Christmas Island phosphate deposits, and in 1948 the Australian and New Zealand governments purchased the assets of the Christmas Island Phosphate Company. However, with the high freight costs, the United Kingdom Government would remain an occasional buyer.

The BPC was also encountering increasing problems with the local Nauru community and rehabilitation efforts to get mining back to normal on the Island. At the same time, Banaba was a very different story. With the Banabans already removed to Rabi in Fiji, the BPC now had Banaba under their complete control. But the feelings of the Banabans were no less than that of the Nauruans, which would become very apparent in the years ahead.

# 10. Australia and Nauru under a new Trusteeship Agreement

Even though the Mandate over Nauru had been granted to the British Empire, Australia had remained the administering authority by agreement with Britain and New Zealand. Now with Nauru under the spotlight Australia in consultation with New Zealand, proposed that there should be an international conference to establish a SouthSeas Regional Commission for the future development of Oceania. This idea was rejected; instead, compromises were made for each country to frame Trusteeship Agreements.

By January 1946, Australia, on behalf of the other partners in the Commission, stated to the General Assembly of the United Nations that an appropriate trusteeship agreement for Nauru would soon be forthcoming. However, this was a far more difficult task, with the Commissioner's conflict of interest over human rights issues relating to the indigenous community and BPC staff.

Another threat was soon to emerge, with Australia pressing for total responsibility over the administration of Nauru. The British Foreign Office was more inclined to support the Australian proposal. It had grave concerns over the bad impression United Kingdom would suffer trying to hold on to a small remote Pacific Island when it had far more important territories to worry about. Back in London, there were other concerns over the conflict with Article 76(d) of the United Nations Charter. The Nauru Agreement contradicted with the Charter of the International Trade Organisation.

On October 4 1947, a draft Trusteeship Agreement was read to the Sub-Committee of the General Assembly. It surprisingly was approved with hardly a mention of the Commissioners, phosphate, monopolies or economic exploitation.

Now with growing animosity towards Colonial authority and the insistence by the United Nations for '...the equality of all peoples irrespective of race, colour, religionor sex and a determination to protect backward people from so-called exploitation ...' (William and Macdonald 1985:363).

The British Phosphate Commissioners knew they could no longer ignore these issues. They had to make a great effort to avoid anything that could embroil them in accusations of racial discrimination.

Although the Nauruans were never involved in any of these negotiations, they soon learned to take a vital interest in the United Nations and use it to their advantage. The Nauruans would eventually negotiate increased phosphate payments with a portion to be paid into a new

Community Long Term Investment Fund. They used the Banaban Provident Fund, initially established in 1931, as their model. The Nauru situation only added to fuel the unrest with the Banabans, who were now on Rabi. However, the Banaban's decision to remain on Rabi permanently had still not been made. While government officials and the Commissioners were keen to have the Banabans permanently out of the way, a Colonial Office official was more candid in his views:

> 'The Banabans have, of course, plenty of money, and if only their present distress can be used as a means of persuading them to leave their island home, one of the most awkward problems of the Gilbert and Ellice Island Colony will have been solved, and the B.P.C. can be left to work their own sweet will on Ocean Island until the time when, about 45 years after the end of the War, there will be nothing left but a few limestone pinnacles sticking above the water' (William and Macdonald 1985:364).

Now all these years later and with the Banabans ignorant of the plans to have them permanently removed to Rabi and their homeland mined away to nothing, these words are a true inditement of what would occur.

By April 1947, as Banaban resentment grew, Colonial officials were directed not to give them any advice on land matters. The Banabans, now on their own and with no independent legal advice, negotiated a new agreement with the BPC based on determining traditional Banaban landowners' boundaries. However, the Commission had completely underestimated the landowners believing that the six Banaban leaders and their wives would be able to return to the Island and confirm these details.

Instead, over half of the Banaban population decided to go to Banaba under their rights as individual landholders within their cultural law known as *te rii ni Banaba* (Sigrah and King 2001:62).

With a critical referendum looming where the Banabans would have the right to decide their future, the Commissioners had no choice but to approve such an excessive request. As far as the Commissioners were concerned, the Banabans had to remain on Rabi. While the Banabans believed that they could live on Rabi and would be freely able to travel back and forward to their homeland. On May 13, the Banabans decided to make Rabi their permanent home. The votes were 270 'for' and only 48 'against' (Maude 1946).

# 11. The differences between Banaba, Nauru and Christmas Islands under the British Phosphate Commission

During the 1950s, the differences between the BPC's financial obligations and their operations on the three phosphate islands became very apparent. On Christmas Island, the Commission paid the actual cost of administration via the Christmas Island Phosphate Commission. On Nauru, the Commissioners had to meet the cost of administration as well as pay royalty payments to the Nauruan landowners who lived on the Island. These royalty payments were more politically motivated to ease the increasing pressure from the United Nations.

It was a completely different case on Banaba, with the Island administratively linked with the Gilbert and Ellice Island Colony since the first discovery of phosphate on Banaba. Initially, after many complaints and protests from the Pacific Phosphate Company and then the BPC, the phosphate industry had been used to fund an otherwise improvised colony for the British Government. To further complicate the situation, the small Banaban population had been moved to Rabi under the much larger colony of Fiji. With funding in short supply for public works and social services, the British and Fiji Governments believed they could not cause a precedent by treatingthe Banabans differently from the thousands of Indian immigrants already livingin Fiji. With the Banabans virtually left on their own and with just a solitary adviser, Banaban discontent only escalated.

During May 1963 negotiations, the Banabans realised that the British Government had no intentions of looking after their affairs. The Banabans had dealt directly with the BPC in the past land negotiations. Now the Commissioners were barred from dealing directly with them. It had already been suggested before the 1965 negotiations that,

> '... if the partner governments were not prepared to provide for the future of the Banabans from the levies paid to the Gilbert and Ellice Island Colony, that the Commissioners should make some provision for the Banabans on a long term basis. A levy of 2 shillings per ton for the lifetime of the deposits to produce a capital fund of some £900 000 was proposed that would give the Banaban community an income of £45 000 in perpetuity and still leave the Commissioner free to deal in theirjudgement with the needs of the Banabans and continue to make some provision

for their current wellbeing' (Williams and Macdonald 1985: 494).

Back in London, U.K. Commissioner Sir Alexander Waddell was constantly trying to bring the issue to the attention of the Colonial Office and found it difficult to find anyone who would accept responsibility for the Banabans. The United Kingdom sought to more than double the existing levies via taxation to support the funding of the Colony.

The Banabans argued they 'were the most unfortunate people in the world' who had suffered hardship, disappointment and misery. They claimed that 'the next generation will suffer badly when the phosphate ends'.

The Australian and New Zealand Governments saw the Banabans as the responsibility of the United Kingdom Government. At the same time, the UK government stood firm in its resolve NOT to allocate any funds to the Banabans at the expense of the Gilbert and Ellice Islands Colony.

During a visit to Banaba in October 1967, the Banabans raised issues over the replanting of mined-out lands while they also tried to obstruct mining operations. Arguments also emanated between the Banabans and the Gilbert and Ellice Island labourers over the rights to Banaba's phosphate revenue and Banaba's place within the Colony.

In April 1968, the Banabans officially approached the United Nations for the immediate return of Banaba to their control and political independence, including a stop to any increase of output from the mining operations. They also insisted on immediate and complete rehabilitation of all worked-out areas on the Island.

Just months prior, on January 31 1968, the Nauruans finally celebrated independence and formed the new Nauru Phosphate Corporation. With the loss of Nauru from BPC control, much more pressure was placed on the operations on Banaba. It soon became apparent that the United Kingdom did not share the same views as the other two governments over Banaba and the Christmas Island operations. While Australian and New Zealand Governments lobbied to try and gain more control over the BPC management.

The decolonisation of Nauru had created a precedent for the Gilbert and Ellice Islands Colony and the Banabans. The sale of the BPC operations on Nauru caused conflict between the three partner governments. The Commissioners received around $12 million and disagreed over distributing the surplus funds between the partners.

# 12. The legal responsibilities of the British Phosphate Commissioners

By November 1971, with all these major developments with the Nauruans, the discontent of the Banabans came to the fore. The Banabans issued writs for $120 million against the United Kingdom Government and the Commissioners. This development again brought the full legal status of the Commissioners into question as individuals and collectively, dating writing back to the original drafting of the NauruAgreement.

The British Phosphate Commission had never been incorporated; therefore, the sole legal responsibility for the BPC fell on the Commissioners as individuals. This reality now impacted eachCommissioner as they considered the best way to deal with the situation. Two options were considered: one to get the action squashed on the grounds that British courts lacked jurisdiction over agreements signed on Banaba and the other to claim sovereign immunity. This latter defence was based on the grounds of diplomatic immunity for Australia and

New Zealand, arguing that the Banabans writ was against foreign governments.

By 1972 the Commissioners were divided on how they should proceed. With the Australian Government's full backing, Sir Allen Brown, the Australia Commissioner, wanted to pursue all possible forms of defence, including trying to get the actions struck off. The British position was that the case should be allowed to proceed. However, the primary concern of all the Commissioners was the bad publicity the matter could generate to the detriment of the business dealings of the BPC.

The Australian Government feared any sign of weakness could affect their position with the Nauruans, prompting them to pursue court action. The United Kingdomand New Zealand Governments, were more concerned over the political ramifications and embarrassment at the United Nations, Especially if it appeared that the Banabanswere being denied natural justice at the hands of three wealthy nations. It became very apparent to the Commissioners that the Banabans were being driven by an absolute quest for justice and were prepared to pursue the case to the bitter end, regardless of any financial gain.

By 1973 other political developments further complicated the situation and created another precedent when the United Kingdom reluctantly agreed to grant independence to the Ellice Islands in recognition of their nationality within the Colony[4]. This move only added to the resolve of the Banabans to once again seek their independence via the United Nations. As the court case slowly proceeded forward, the Commissioners were keen to reach an out of court settlement, and a figure of $2.5 million was discussed.

The Australian and New Zealand Governments had instructed their Commissioners to 'settle' and were willing to pay much more to maintain goodwill in the South Pacific region. They were also prepared to let the United Kingdom Government go it alone. Australian and New Zealand Governments had received legal advice that certain disclosures could be forthcoming if the case was to proceed andprove very embarrassing to the partner governments.

While the partner governmentsand the Commissioners tried to agree amongst themselves on the best way to deal with the case, the Banabans further extended their fight for sovereignty. In January 1974, they lodged a petition to the British Government for the legal separation of Banaba from the Gilbert and Ellice Islands Colony.

Early in 1975, as formal hearings loomed, the partner governments finally agreed on ajoint attempt for an out of court settlement. This time the negotiation figures had increased from the original $2.5 million to $4 million, with another $1 million kept in reserve on the proviso that the partner governments would not accept

---

[4] This would eventually lead to the formal separation of the Ellice Islands from the Colony in 1978becoming the independent Republic of Tuvalu.

any liability. While the Commissioners tried to reach an out of court settlement with the Banabans separately from the partner governments, their offer to the Banabans amounted in total to $1.25 million. The Banabans rejected this offer because the Commissioners could not offer any political concessions, which were solely under the control of the United Kingdom Government. The Banabans legal proceedings continued in the courts.

Behind the scenes, the day-to-day running of BPC's operations on Banaba were also becoming more difficult. There was a downturn in the world demand for fertiliser, and the Commissioners had to borrow heavily from their mounting stockpiles. There was also growing hostility by Colony officials toward the duty-free BPC trade store and the growing replacement of expatriate staff by Islanders. The Gilbert Islands demanded more control over policy as the Colony moved closer to independence.

The court case hearings were finally completed on June 1976, and on November 29, Judge Megarry delivered his judgment. The royalty claim against the United Kingdom Government was dismissed because it had acted according to the law. While the claims of destroying Banaban cemeteries were dismissed and described as 'stupidly and offensively false'. The claims relating to over mining of Banaban land failed because title had not been proved. On the replanting action, the judge found against the BPC but could not offer a figure because of the high costs involved in replanting and instructed the Commissioners and Banabans to reach a settlement.

Again the original offer of $1.25 million was offered and again rejected. The parties returned to the judge. Again with instructions from the judge, the Banabans eventuallyaccepted the offer, which would at least cover some of their mounting legal costs.

In his summation, the judge pointed out the grave breaches of the United Kingdom Government in fixing royalties in 1931 and the failure to provide advice to the Banabans before the 1947 negotiations. The judge also instructed that in the case of the Banabans, 'he could not right what he considered was a wrong and left it to the Crown to do what it considered to be proper' (Binder 1978:165).

Following the judge's direction, the United Kingdom Government dispatched Richard Posnett, aformer colonial governor to investigate the situation. His findings focused on two main issues, mainly the Banabans continuing claim against the United Kingdom over lost royalties between 1920 and 1977 and their demand for sovereignty over Banaba.Over the next two years, his efforts to bring about a resolution between all parties was still unresolved. With the Gilbert Islands opposing Banaban independence and Posnett aware of the future economic problems looming for the Banabans, he made the following recommendation. The sum of $7 million of the BPC's accumulated surpluses should be used to establish a fund for the development of Rabi. By May 1977, in addition to any settlement reached with the BPC, the Banabans would be offered an ex gratia payment of $10 million, subject to no further legal action being entered into. The Banabans held out from accepting the settlement as they still lobbied and argued over sovereignty.

Concerning Banaban sovereignty, again, the British Government washed their hands of the Banabans and added a final nail in the coffin by handing over all responsibility for the decision to the newly formed Council of Ministers had been introduced along with the Colony's new constitution. Unfortunately, the Council believed Banaba was an integral part of the Gilbert Islands and would oppose any talk of separation or independence for the Banabans 'either now or in the future' (Sigrah and King 2001:18). It was not until October 1978 that the Banabans and Gilbertese finally began formal discussions over the winddown of the phosphate industry on Banaba and the disposal of assets.

The Gilbert Islands were finally granted independence on July 1979 and became the Republic of Kiribati. Special provisions were made in the newly formed constitution for the allocation of two Banaban seats in the Kiribati legislature. One representative from Banaba and the other from Rabi in Fiji, and the return of land previously held by the BPC back to the original Banaban landowners.

# 13. Final close to phosphate mining

As the final load of phosphate left Banaba on November 25 1979, the BPC left allthe machinery and plant behind on the Island as it was more expensive to remove it. The Kiribati Government was given the rights to all the removable fittings on the Island. Asthe Banabans watched their hospital and other key buildings being stripped bare byKiribati Government authorities, they were left with a fully operating mining plant and a powerhouse they did not know how to use for their small population. They were also left with the curse of phosphate reserves that the Kiribati Government viewed as a highly viable asset in the future when more modern mining technology was available.

After the mining ceased on Banaba, the BPC made major development grants available from their surpluses to the Republic of Kiribati and the Republic of Tuvalu. The end of phosphate mining had a devastating impact on the local economy. The Banabans had held out from accepting any settlement from their court case for as long as possible while the loss of phosphate royalties impacted their small community. So it was not until four years after the court case ended that they finally accepted a settlement. Over that period, with the money held in trust and earning high interest, the final amount had risen by another $4 million. For the Banabans, accepting this final settlement was the last blow to their morale (Teai 1997).

For all the past years of their mammoth struggle and belief 'that they were in the right and God would help them, they were left entirely on their own and isolated on Rabi. There would be no development or future grants to help them establish Rabi or to rehabilitate their homeland. The reality of the situation hit as the $10 million settlement and interest were put in a trust fund for perpetuity. They now had to support their whole community on the interest generatedincome.

The matter had finally come to a close for Australia and the other partner governments. After 80 years of phosphate mining, over 20 million tons of Banaban land had been removed, with most of the soil being scattered to the winds of Australia's farmlands.

In 1997 in a private meeting between the author and the Australian High Commissioner in Kiribati, the Australian Government's position on the Banabans was conveyed. As far as the Australian Government was concerned, the matter over the Banabans was dead and buried as soon as they accepted the British courts' payment. As the author was in the country assisting in the making of aBanaban documentary for national broadcast in Japan, the Australian Government was more concerned about the bad publicity the story could generate with one of their major trading nations. These candid comments from the Commissioner also endorsed Australia's official diplomatic view that the issue of the Banabans had been dealt with and put to rest and preferred it would stay that way.

For the Australian Government, the major contribution of the Banabans over the past century in building a wealthy farming nation is now less than a memory. In Australia, the Banabans are regarded as the forgotten people of the Pacific.

7. Devastating impact of phosphate mining by 1932.

8. The ongoing destruction of Banaba by phosphate mining by 1968.

# 14. Summary

The history of the Banabans, the near destruction of their Island, and their identity through phosphate mining is complex, involving major political players, worldevents, and the halcyon days of British Colonial rule in the Pacific. Other significant issues raised by this period of history include environmental degradation, pollution, denial of basic human rights and cultural identity. The remoteness of Banaba and its small indigenous population of only 450 people situated on one the world's largest phosphate deposits made the Banabans expendable. They received no recognition for the economic benefits their island could bring to the rest of the developed world.

Western ideals of money and management roles within the Banaban community were never part of cultural understanding. Yet, with limited knowledge of these commercial principles and no grasp of world politics, the Banabans tried every avenue possible to save their homeland. Now over forty years later, there has been no effort to rehabilitate Banaba, not even a study to investigate what is possible. Yet over the past decade, the

Kiribati Government has put money and resources into the feasibility of re-mining the Island.

Life on Rabi, the island where the Banabans were relocated to following the devastating effects of phosphate mining on their home island, has become increasingly challenging for the community. Limited economic opportunities and a lack of basic infrastructure have made it difficult for the Banabans to sustain their traditional way of life. As a result, many Banabans have been forced to seek better opportunities for their families by either moving to other areas of Fiji or migrating to Kiribati or abroad.

As stated in a United Nations International Human Rights report (2002: Section38), 'since the 1980s all indicators for the social well-being of the community have shown a serious decline'. The Banabans forced removal from their homeland and subsequent resettlement on Rabi has caused immense cultural and social disruption for the Banabans, who are struggling to maintain their identity and sense of belonging in the face of ongoing challenges.

Meanwhile, the Kiribati Government has built on their Revenue Equalization Reserve Fund, initially set up for them in 1956 from accumulated Banaban phosphate royalties. As of 2021, the Fund is valued at nearly US$960 million (https://globalswf.com/fund/RERF). On December 20 2005, the Banabans carried amotion in the Kiribati Parliament to consider giving part of the trust fund as a pensionto Rabi Islanders, who were over seventy years old. The motion was rejected, and the Banabans threatened:

> 'Banaba Island belongs to the Rabi people, not to the Kiribati Government. We must now consider giving the re-mining rights to the Fiji Government' (FijiTimes 2005).

The response by the Kiribati Government on December 23 2005, highlights a pattern of British government policies and protocols that have been passed on to distance any responsibility or blame for issues facing the Banabans:

> 'The Kiribati Government would only grant such gratuities if Rabi islanders wanted to move back to Kiribati … the Kiribati Government would very much like to grant the Rabi Islanders access to these social benefits if they decide to go back to Kiribati' (Fiji Times 2005).

This issue also highlighted the grievances still held by the Banabans and the complete lack of support from within the Kiribati Government:

Teitirake Corrie, a Rabi Council of Leaders member and the Banaban people's link to the Kiribati Parliament stated that his people wanted to sever ties with the Kiribati Government and cede their original home, Banaba, to Fiji. In Kiribati Parliament, he asked,

> 'The Kiribass [Kiribati] Parliament to pay the original inhabitants of Banaba 40 dollars a month in pensions. They say the Kiribati Government refuses to pay pensions to their elders, even though the money is from phosphate royalties from mining on Banaba. Of the five

thousand Banabans in Fiji, less than one hundred are over seventy years old and qualify for the Kiribati Government's pension scheme". Corrie says their case is genuine since the money in the Kiribass [Kiribati] government reserves is from Banaban phosphate mining royalties. Corrie says he told the Kiribass [Kiribati] Parliament that his elders did not move from their original home of their own free will but were forced out by the British during World War 2 in 1945. The Rabi Council of Leaders will meet in the first week of February to decide how to take the issue further' (Fiji TV News 2006).

The Kiribati Government was never privy or involved with the decision making in the setting up of the Banaban trust funds based on their royalty payments and exorbitant taxation schemes relating to Banaban phosphate. They were complicit in their rejection of Banaban sovereignty and their efforts for independence. Yet with growing reserves in the RERF and Banaba under Kiribati control, the Banabans are remiss that none of these funds generated from their Island has been put back into some type of regeneration scheme or bettering the lives of the landowners back in Rabi, and those living on Banaba today.

The Banaban population is currently a dying one, and there would be only a small number of landowners now over the age of 70 still alive today. The rejection of such a token gesture and the frustrated calls to hand over re-mining rights to the Fiji Government only add to the growing and building level of Banaban discontent today.

While Australia and the other partner governments haggled over the financial gains and their rights to subsidised phosphate for their farmers, the interference between the role of the British Phosphate Commissioners and their perspective Governments began to merge and could not remain impartial. From introducing compulsory land acquisitions and writing laws that would make life for the Banabans more restrictive under the cloak of civil law and order, the original privately owned Company and then the BPC had the power and backing behind it when required.

As the British Government floundered trying to finance their remote and vast Pacific Island Colony, the revenue generated from phosphate mining on Banaba would relieve Britain of the financial responsibility for administering the Gilbert and Ellice Protectorate (later Colony).

Banaban phosphate royalties were eventually distributed 85% to the Gilbert and Ellice Islands and a small 15% to the Banabans.

The final distribution rates of Banaban phosphate:
- Australian farmers received 66% (or 13.2 million tons) of cheap phosphate.
- New Zealand farmers received 28% (or 5.6 million tons) of cheap phosphate.
- Great Britain received 4% or 800,000 tons of phosphate at 50% of the price paid by Europeans.

As clearly seen in the final figures, there is no denying the Australian Government's physical and economic gains were at a great loss to the Banaban people.

The partner governments, especially the United Kingdom, which had absolute control over the decision and law-making of the Colony and the Banabans. To the relief of the Australian and New Zealand Governments, they were relieved to hand over the entire future of the Banabans and their homeland to the Kiribati Government and the Fiji Government, who now had the bulk of the Banaban population residing on Rabi.

The Banaban calls to rehabilitate Banaba are not unreasonable, especially when the Australian Government, through auspices of the Australian Nature Conservation Agency (ANCA), have worked on rehabilitating Christmas Island.

The Commission's other phosphate island in the consortium is known as the Christmas Island Rainforest Rehabilitation Program (CIRRP). Christmas, unlike Banaba, was never home to an indigenous people, but its rainforests offer the only home for the Abbott's Booby bird and the birthplace of millions of red crabs.

On Christmas, the project was a joint venture of collaboration between the Christmas Island Phosphate Mining Company, ANCA and the Island's mining union. Yet this very positive step by the Australian Government only highlights the complete lack of regard for the Banaban people and their devastated Island (Hart 1995).

# 13. Conclusion

While the Australian Government has successfully distanced itself from the entire Banaba situation, it cannot deny its role in destroying it and neglecting its people. Furthermore, under the current political sphere of the Banabans, now a minority people or Fourth World People (McCall 2004) split under the governance of two third-world nations, the Australian Government now has the luxury of wiping its hands of the Banabans completely in today's world.

Over the past decades of the author's involvement in sourcing aid and development projects for the two Banaban communities, these restraints are constantly present. The Australian Government cannot be directly approached, and when they are, all aid requests for Rabi must go through the Fiji Government and the Kiribati Government for Banaba. This usually makes these requests nearly impossible through the proper diplomatic channels.

The Australian Government argues that under their foreign policy, they cannot recognise the Banabans under their community status.

The Banabans are calling on the Australian Government to officially recognise the historical contribution the Banaban Community has made to Australia's agriculture industry over the past century. There are various ways in which this could be achieved as an offer of good faith for the Banabans' role in Australian history:

- Offer direct scholarships and educational and technical training to Banaban youth.
- To recognise Banaban cultural status and identity within the Republics of Fiji and Kiribati and relaxation of strict visa requirements for those Banabans travelling under Fiji passports to Australia.
- Offer aid and development projects directly via AusAid and Rabi Council of Leaders for Rabi and Banaba Islands.
- Major areas of immediate concern on Rabi:
  Improvement of housing and public buildings, especially regarding continued and devastating damage caused by multiple cyclones, education, communications, and health. Public works and infrastructure, including village electrification, inter-village transport and community-based buildings.
- To support Banaban efforts by lobbying the Kiribati Government and the partner governments involved in mining Banaba to fund and conduct feasibility studies for Banaba's rehabilitation.

While Banaba remains in a neglected state with people living amongst the asbestos ruins of the old mining industry, the Island can only support a small population between 350 to 500 people on the 150 acres remaining unmined. With most Banabans living on Rabi and no industry or future likely on the Island, the Australian Government must help the Banabans overcome this immediate crisis.

Major areas of immediate concern:
- Lack of clean drinking water due to prolonged droughts.
- Regular inter-island shipping to secure food supplies.

In all probability, Australia and the other partner governments believe the Banabans are a dying race that will soon be fully absorbed into mainstream life in Kiribati andalso Fiji. This was the original mistake that was made back in 1900 when Albert Ellisfirst arrived on the Island and started making complicated contractual arrangementswith a lone Banaban man he perceived as King.

The fight for justice over the past century has been inbred into each new generation. While daily life is a struggle, upholding Banaban identity and the quest to return to the homeland will remain.

In the future, staging a Banaban Forum to formally invite all the past and present political players to sit around the table and discuss the problems facing the community and seek workable solutions as a collective group is needed. It is essential for Banaban leaders to proactively take their past and present grievances to the countries responsible for the position they are in today. It is also imperative to finally put a stop to the shuffling and side-stepping of responsibility that these governments have all used over the past and present century.

In the final draft, Australia was and still is, regardless of any political justification, the main beneficiary of Banaban phosphate. At the very least, it owes the Banabans full recognition for their role in shaping Australia as a nation of over 25 million people and the quality of life enjoyed by all Australians today.

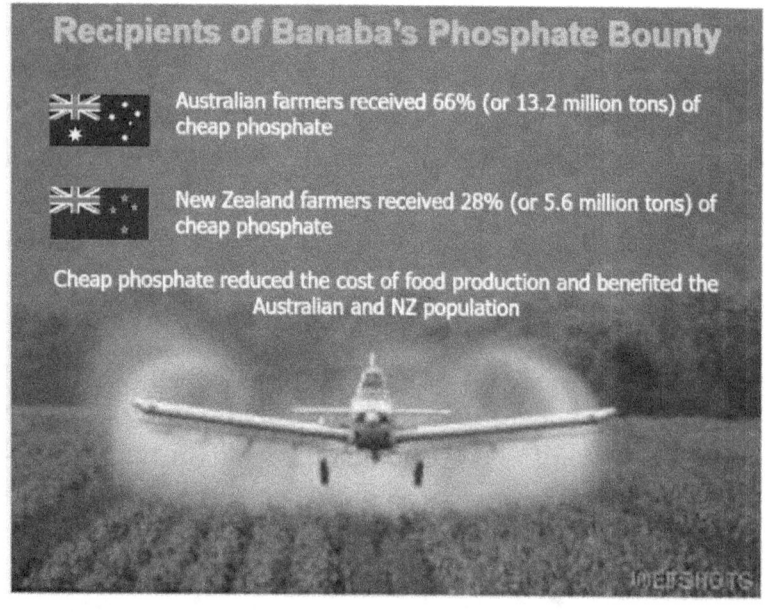

9. Australia was the primary recipient of Banaba's phosphate.

# References

Anon. 2005a. *Mining History of Lady Musgrave Island.* [Online]. Available: http://www.workingpapers.org.country/kiribati.htm [November 25 2005]

Anon. 2005b. Ellis, Sir Albert Fuller. *Encyclopaedia of New Zealand 1966.* [Online]. Available: https://teara.govt.nz/en/1966/ellis-sir-albert-fuller [November 25 2005]

Anon. 2005c. Ellis, Sir Albert Fuller. *Dictionary of New Zealand 1966.* [Online]. Available: http://www.dnzb.govt.nz/dnzb/Print_Essay.asp [November 25 2005]

Anon. 2005d. *Working Paper Sites of Political Science: Country Biography Index.* [Online]. Available: http://www.lmcruises.com.au/en/mining.htm [November 29 2005]

Anon. 2005e. Coral Sea Island. *Encyclopaedia Britannica.* [Online]. Available: http://www.britannica.com/eb/article-9026233 [November 29 2005]

Anon. 2005f. *Documenting Democracy. Queensland Coast Island Act 1897 (Qld).* [Online]. Available: http://www.foundingdocs.gov.au/item.asp?dID=65 [29November2005]

Anon. 2005g. IMF Concludes 2001 Article IV Consultation with Kiribati. International Monetary Fund. Public information Notice: (Pin) No. 01/96. September 21, 2001. [Online]. Available: http://www.imf.org/external/np/sec/pn/2001/pn0196.htm [December 20 2005]

AUSTRALIA. Foreign Affairs Defence and Trade References Committee. August 2003. *A Pacific engaged*

*Australia's relations with Papua New Guinea and the island states of the south-west Pacific.* Canberra: Senate Printing Unit, Parliament House, Canberra.

Binder, Pearl. *Treasure Islands – The trials of the Banabans.* Sydney: Angus andRobertson Ltd, 1978.

Ellis, A.F. *Adventuring in the Coral Seas.* Sydney: Angus and Robertson Ltd, 1936. Ellis, A.F. *Ocean Island and Nauru.* Sydney: Angus and Robertson Ltd, 1936.

Ellis, A.F. *Mid-Pacific Outposts.* Auckland: Brown and Stewart, 1946.Grimble, A. *A Pattern of Islands.* London: John Murray, 1952.

Hart, R. 1995. The Unholy Alliance on Christmas Island, Part One. *Banaba/OceanIsland News,* (15):1-3, May/June.

Hart, R. 1995. The Unholy Alliance on Christmas Island, Part Two. *Banaba/OceanIsland News,* (16):2-3, July/August.

H.E. Governor-General Australia. 1927. Letter to the Right Honourable the Secretary of State for Dominion Affairs, October 22. [Original copy in records of Australian Archives, Canberra.]

Hindmarsh, Gerard. *One Minority People – A Report on the Banabans,* Commissioned by UNESCO, Apia. November, 2002.

Kiribati Government would only grant gratuities if Rabi islanders wanted to move back to Kiribati. 2005. *Fiji Times/Pacnews.* December 23.

Kiribati Legislation – *The Constitution of Kiribati.* Pacific Law Materials.

Lampert, R.J. *Anthropological Investigation of te Aka Village, Ocean Island: Preliminary Report.* Canberra, Department of Anthropology, Australian NationalUniversity, 1965. [Not for publication]

Lampert, R.J. *An Anthropological Investigation of Te Aka Village, Ocean Island: Preliminary Report.* Canberra, Department of Anthropology, Australian National University, 1965. [Not for publication].

Lampert, R.J. An Anthropological Investigation of Ocean Island, Central Pacific.
*Archaeology and Physical Anthropology in Oceania*, Vol. 111, No.1. April, 1968

Langdon, Robert. 1966. *The Ocean Islanders - a quite scandalous document.* in: New Guinea and Australia, the Pacific and South-East Asia 1(4), 42-52, 1966. (The story ofPhosphate exploitation on Ocean I. and the publication of the document of May 3 1900, stating the conditions upon which the British Phosphate Commission could operate) (see Inder, Stuart 1966, Part 2).

Mahaffy, A. 1910. Ocean Island. *Blackwood's Magazine.* November.

Maude, Harry and Honor. 1997. Interview conducted by authors November 1997.Canberra. [Cassette recording in possession of authors.]

Maude, H.C. and H.E. The Social Organisation of Banaba or Ocean Island of Banabaor Ocean Island, Central Pacific, *Journal of the Polynesian Society* 41, 1932.

Maude, H.C. and H.E. *The Book of Banaba.* Institute of Pacific Studies, University ofSouth Pacific Fiji, 1995

Maude, H.E. *Memorandum on the Future of the Banaban Population of Ocean Island; With Special Relations to their Lands and Funds.* Chief Lands Commissioner, Gilbert and Ellice Islands Colony, 1946.

NEW ZEALAND. House of Representatives. 1919. Nauru and Other Phosphate Islands in the Pacific. Auckland: Government Printer.

O'Brien, Sir George. Telegram transcript from Office of the High Commissioner for the Western Pacific, Suva Fiji, to Colony Office London, February 1900.

Rabi community lays claim to Ocean Island. 2006. *Fiji TV News.* January 1. Rabi considers mining options. 2005. *Fiji Times.* December 19.

Sigrah, Raobeia Ken and King, Stacey M. *Te Rii ni Banaba.* IPS, University of South Pacific Fiji, 2001.

Tai, Tomas. 1997. Interview with Island Magistrate by S. King Rabi, Fiji. 1997. [unrecorded].

UNITED NATIONS. International Human Rights Instruments: *Core document forming part of the reports of States Parties,* Fiji. 2002. Dist. General. Original: English.

Williams, Maslyn and Macdonald, Barrie. *The Phosphateers.* Melbourne University Press. 1985.

# Appendix 1: Letter from Prime Minster of Australia to Right Honourable the Secretary of State for Dominion Affairs, dated October 22 1927.

**COMMONWEALTH OF AUSTRALIA.**

**GOVERNOR-GENERAL'S OFFICE**

DECODE of telegram despatched by H.E. the Governor-General to the Rt.Hon. the Secretary of State for Dominion Affairs, dated 22nd October, '27

S.

Following from Prime Minister begins –

British Phosphate Commission. Australian Commissioner has informed us regarding course of negotiations for land at Ocean Island required by Commissioners. They consider basis for acquiring 150 acres phosphate land proposed by Commissioners in letter to you of 16th December 1926 was equitable and even liberal and they might reasonably have declined to improve their offer but in July last an amended basis was agreed at Ocean Island between the Resident Commissioner and the Chief Representative of the British Phosphate Commissioners which was approved by the Commissioners in order to show their desire to meet as far as possible the views of the Banabans as represented by the Resident Commissioner. Understand this amended basis was approved also by you and represented the maximum payments to which the Commissioners could agree. Phosphate is vitally important to Australia and as the phosphate from Ocean Island is urgently required now and will in future be required in progressively increasing quantities for use in Australia and other countries within the Empire it is important that no restrictions shall prevent the development and working of the deposits to the best advantage by the Commissioners. The terms offered by the Commissioners are in excess of those recently agreed at Nauru and amply cover the differences in conditions between that Island and Ocean Island providing both for the present and the future welfare of the Banabans. As all the phosphate on Ocean Island will eventually be required it appears to Commissioners advisable that steps should be taken to secure another island or islands for the use of the Banabans when Ocean Island is no longer suitable for their habitation and the Commissioners have expressed their willingness to co-operate in this matter. The question of immediate removal to another island can be avoided if the land now required is made available without restrictive terms and conditions. As the Banabans are asking excessive payments for other land which the Commissioners now require to lease for the construction of new works urgently necessary to ensure increased output it is desirable that equitable terms and conditions should now be agreed for at least 20 years as at Nauru for leasing land required for purposes other than phosphate mining.

Commissioners therefore request that

(a) phosphate mining land at Ocean Island be made available without delay for use as required by the British Phosphate Commissioners upon terms not exceeding those agreed at Ocean Island early in July and approved by the Commissioners and the Colonial Office;

(b) terms and conditions for leasing land at Ocean Island for purpose other than phosphate mining be arranged for 20 years on the same basis as at Nauru;

(c) that it be recognised that the whole deposit of phosphate at Ocean Island must eventually be worked;

(d) that arrangements be made for the acquisition of another island or islands suitable for eventual occupation by the Banabans.

As you have doubtless been advised in similar terms by United Kingdom Commissioner shall be glad to hear your views. My Government concurs generally with recommendation but considers the suggested transfer of Banabans to another island raises somewhat serious issues. We do not consider we are justified in making such a recommendation as this matter is one entirely within the province of British Administration. Ends.

# About the Author

Stacey M. King is a historian, author, entrepreneur, and philanthropist. She has been an advocate for the indigenous Banaban people for many decades.

In 1989, she began researching her family's history for a historical novel based on their lives titled – *Nakaa's Awakening: Land of Matang* (Book One; 2000).

In 1997, she formed a personal and collaborative partnership with the late Ken Raobeia Sigrah, a Banaban Clan historian and spokesperson. Their first published work, *Te Rii Ni Banaba - backbone of Banaba* (2001; 2019), is a history book written from an indigenous perspective and endorsed by Banaban Clan elders.

With the establishment of Banaban Vision Publications, Stacey is converting much of their writings and research findings into digital publications. Since the passing of her beloved partner, Raobeia Ken Sigrah, she is determined to continue his legacy in preserving Banaban history for future generations.

# Other Titles By The Author

**Banaban History Non-Fiction Book**
*Te Rii ni Banaba*. First Edition: IPS, Suva, Fiji. 2001, Second edition, Banaban Vision Publications, Gold Coast, Australia 2019.
*Australia Banaba Relations: the price of shaping a nation*, Banaban Vision, Gold Coast, March 2023.

**History Non-Fiction Book – Chapter in Book**
The Banaba-Ocean Island chronicles: private collections, indigenous record-keeping, fact and fiction. Chapter 17, *Hunting the collectors*. Cambridge Scholars, UK.

**Historical Fiction**
*Nakaa's Awakening, Land of Matang.* Banaban Vision Publications, Gold Coast, Australia, 2020 (Book 1; 4-book series. Blend of history, biography and fictional reconstruction)

**Articles and Presentations**
Australia Banaba Relations: the price of shaping a nation is now a call for recognition

Banaba-Ocean Island Chronicles: Private collections and indigenous record-keeping proving fact from fiction
Cultural Identity of Banabans
Legacy of a Miners Daughter and Assessment of the Social Changes of the Banabans after Phosphate Mining on Banaba
Essentially Being Banaban in Today's World: The role of Banaban Law, Te Rii Ni Banaba (Backbone of Banaba) in a Changing World

**Banaban Social Media sites by Authors**
Abara Banaba–Come Meet the Banabans: banaban.com
Banaban Vision: banabanvision.com
Banaban Voice Facebook: facebook.com/groups/banabanvoice/
Banaban Vision Blog: banabanvoice.ning.com/
Banaban Vision: banabanvision.com
Banaban Media: vocalmedia.com

**Connect with Us:**
Banaban Vision Publications
PO Box 1116 Paradise Point Qld 4216 Australia
Stacey M. King – Author's Page: staceymking.com
Email: admin@banaban.com
Te Rii Ni Banaba -Facebook group:
https://www.facebook.com/groups/296299534653304/
Linkedin: Ken Sigrah:
https://www.linkedin.com/in/ken-sigrah-821b5975/
Linkedin: Stacey King:
https://www.linkedin.com/in/stacey-king-4ba68a76/

www.ingramcontent.com/pod-product-compliance
Lightning Source LLC
Chambersburg PA
CBHW071840290426
44109CB00017B/1878